I guess I'm not really sure how to start all this. I just want to say family who supported me for the months that this book was being made. I'm really proud of myself and of these works and I'm glad I get to share them this way. I hope that these poems give you the same feelings that they gave me, or that you read them and develop your own meaning from them. The beautiful thing about all poetry is that it's open for interpretation so feel free to see them however you do. Let the words speak to your heart like they do mine.

Thank you.
Robert Maxie Jr

To a friend

You're all I have left
The last piece of a broken heart beating in my chest
The best chance I have
An iron lance in my back
To a friend
I'm fighting for you
Dying for you
Lying for you
Telling people I'm alive
When I'm dying because of you
To a friend
You're my last vestige of humanity
The shadow of creeping insanity
You hold me together barely
You tear me apart scarily
I'm fairly certain
I'm falling because of you
Falling for you
To a friend
Don't leave me
You keep me whole
And yet
You made this hole in my chest
My best bet was bested my my best friends hatred
To a friend
You're both sides of one coin
In my wallet
Both ends of one socket

A lightning strike
Your so shocking
Locking, Me in a twisted state of mind I swear my, Mind is cracking
under your weight
You keep me grounded like a paper weight You drag me down
Like an iron weight in water
Drowning or suffocating
Sleep or slaughter
Fed or fodder
Either way you end me
You begin me
Oblivious to what you made
Your destruction has razed or raised me We'll see
To a friend

Convey

I don't want to force feed you my feelings
But I'm feeling like I can't convey
I can't say the things I feel
But I can't play it off either
I'd rather write it down
Put my pains on paper
So they don't make a sound
Though it doesn't matter how loud
Most people are tone deaf
They couldn't hear me calling
Guess they must be phone deaf
They can come back later to collect whatever is left
If they want to listen
If they want to pay attention

It seems like what they do hear
Is not understood
They only know my bad side
Never my good
But if someone needed me to listen
I would
Cause everyone says they want to be heard
But they never listen
They want others to hear their words
But others words
Are like chirping birds
Incessant and unnecessary
And easily ignored
Washed out by the sound
Of their own roar
They only hear what they want
Never the truth
Despite the proof
They have blind eyes
And deaf ears

Broken

I...I just feel broken-hearted
Broken
Alone
I've lost all hope
I'm praying for god to let me go home
Home is where the heart is
My heart is where your heart is
Beating the same beats
Praying the same prayers
Feeling your pain
But I'm just broken
Broken
Broken
Breaking
Like glass

Shattering
Hopeless
Like bleeding doves
Trapped wolves
Screaming at you to listen
Broken
I saw you
Through forests and jungles and deserts I saw you
I was unwanted
Until that first day
That day I changed
I saw hope for my suffering
I saw hope for yours
Here we are
shades
Shadows
Wisps of wind
Mists
Flotsam on vicious waves
A grain of what we used to be
A grain
It's all I need to see of you

Shades

We're just shades
Shadows
Broken frames to our former selves
Cheap knockoffs to the real deal
Old memories of shining steel
Now broken, cracked, rusted, shields
Yielding nothing
Feeling nothing
Saying nothing
Being nothing
But shades
Hidden from the light

Ghosts of a long forgotten past
Phantoms, ghouls, ghosts, unseen

Silence

Silence screams
Yes silence screams
As my mind careens
On the edge of sanity
Dreaming

I'm quietly
Pondering
Wading through dreams and memories
Remembering
As my mind dreams
And silence screams
My lonely dreams
They flee from me
Seeking meaning
In
My silenced screams
Dreaming

Good Enough

Don't let people tell you
Who you are or who you're meant to be
You're meant to be
Perfect in your own imperfect
Way
Twisted, turned, and tweaked
To be how you see fit
How you seem fits
Your own heart's desires
It's not your job to be fuel for society's fires
They're liars
If they say your not good enough
Please
Know your more
Than "good enough

Broken Lights

We are all blind to the truth of this world
Like turtles on a beach
We follow hollow lights
Instead of following our own way
We let ourselves be lead astray
By lights as broken as us
Lights that only feed our lust
To have what we want
Not need
Feed into our dark souls
And for a moment we are consoled
By broken lights
Why
Are we so blind
We know if we follow hollow lights we can only
Die
But We Still go
After those lights
That shine lies
It's a plight
A blight
Of humanity
What we are doing
It's the definition of insanity
Repeat repeat repeat
Wanting different results
Repeat repeat repeat
But we never change
Our faults or ways
We stay the same
Day by day

Yet we pray
For change
Not realizing
God meets us halfway
And it's a shame
We are still to blind to see
Broken lights

Don't Really Matter

I'm trying to find a way
To tell you everything
To tell you what you mean to me
What it means to me
That you're here
Talking to me
Even though I'm worthless
You still think I'm worth it
I don't know why
But I swear I'll try
To be good enough for you
I'm scared
That you don't like me
That I might be
Just a pity case
Just a face
With no meaning
That you're just nice
And I
Don't really matter

Dreaming of clouds

I'm dreaming of clouds
Dreams so loud
That they scream to me
What things mean to me
Truths that I don't see
They take shapes as love and hate
Fear so great
Yet nothing
I dream of hope
I dream of safety
I dream of a world where I don't hate me
Where all my loved ones don't really hate me
My dreams are shaking
Truths so fearsome they're quaking in my mind
Lying eyes watch while I wake and spill the truth in my sleep
Secrets that I keep from myself
Come alive
When I close my eyes

When my mind is allowed to stop blocking me from what I really see
When I don't have to lie to me
To keep myself sane
Because the truths that I know could drive me insane
The clouds take shape to hide my face from fear
To keep my mind clear of what I know is true
That I'm alone
And that really is the least of it

Lies

the lies are what you know
they control you
your words own you
they break you down like glass into a trillion pieces
that don't fit together
because no one ever tells themselves it gets better
we just write ourselves those cursed letters
Shoving lies down our throats
Putting to death our hopes
It's time to speak the truth
And accepting it can only help you
Because lying to yourself ain't working
Only birthing more pain

It's insane
You know you're dying
But not trying to save yourself
Please, save yourself

Deny Deny Deny

Stop asking if I'm fine
I won't ever tell
don't ask why I cried
I'm fine
Why? because I don't want to tell
you don't need to know

i'm being choked
Drowning
Why do I have to hide
behind
my masquerade
why is it so hard
to cry
to let them see
inside
to let them be with me
if I break
If I hold it all in I will shake
and quake
until I finally break
I'm not shy
but I will still
Deny
I'm Broken inside
why
can't I let it out
why am I so stubborn
inside my
heart I can't
show
why
I just
Deny Deny Deny

Rage

It flows in my veins
This venomous rage
Insane saying and ravings
Craving to be heard
Acknowledged
And known
Alone
He stands
Sinking in sands
That no one understands
He's off
In the distance beyond help
Beyond hell
Alone

Stone in a Diamond Mine

Sometimes I feel like a stone in a diamond mine
but it's fine
Though I feel like I'm dying
as a stone in a diamond mine
Is it a crime for me to want more
to do more? To be more?
I feel broken and alone
unwanted with no home
and this is life
for a stone in a diamond mine
But we forget
every diamond was just a stone
alone with no home
but the value is inside the lines
cause we all were once stones in a diamond mine.

Together

How easy do you think this is?
Following you?
Seeing you die?
Seeing you cry?
Watching you fade before my eyes
I swear you're not fine
I swear you're not fine
Look me in my eyes
And don't lie
What do you feel?
Close your eyes what do you see?
Do you see me?
Fighting for you
And losing
I need to save you
So you can save me
Lately
I been falling apart
Trying to hold you together
Get it together
I can't save you
You can't save me
But maybe
Together

We can both get it together
Maybe together

Selfish

Is it really really wrong for me to be selfish
I'm honestly so tired of being selfless
 of caring for myself less
Of thinking of myself less
Not giving myself rest
Letting myself stress
Over other people's trash
Telling myself it's the last time
But this time becomes last time
Time and time again the same rhyme
The same lines
The same lies

Worth it

I'm so tired
I sick of not winning
Of giving my all
But all in all
It's worthless
I'm worthless
I wonder if it's even worth it
All my efforts to be almost perfect
All my work to be something closer
To being good enough
For everyone
Meaningless
Sometimes I just feel like nothing matters
I see no purpose trying
We're all just dying
Turning to dust
And ash
Nothing lasts
And nothing matters
Everything shatters
All things burn

Everything
Is nothing

Dying Fire

I can see the dying fire
In your eyes
But you won't try to survive
You're lying to me
And in your veiled words crying to me
To anyone who can see
To save you
I'm hanging one
While you play your swan songs
Singing of the end
But we just began
It's so insane
I can hear you screaming
Yet you claim
Nothing's wrong

Perspective

There is no lie
There is no truth
Only perspective
Just your perception
Deception inception
Lies and corruption
Broken minds
Instructions
Guiding to destruction
Question your objectives
Learn your instructions
Know thyself
Know thy SELF

Justice

Do you hear that?
The roar
The sound of a billion voices
Raging

Screaming for justice
The rage of the innocent
The dark side of goodness
Fighters
People who stand of freedom
The one thing you cannot ban
Is passion
Passion for justice
Passion for freedom
Passion to fight
Against tyranny
Foolishness

Lie To Me

Please don't lie to me
Do try to be
What I don't need
I don't need
Another heartbreak
Another earth shake
Another earthquake
More pain
I don't need
To be driven insane By you
And the things you do
The way you screw
With my head
The silk soft sound
Of the enticing words you said
Drowning me
Dragging down
Like a weight made of lead
I fear you
More than anything
You terrify me
I want you to stay away
But I don't want you away
I don't wanna be awake
If you're not here to stay
Not to play around with me again
Running circles
Drowning in whirlpools
Typhoons
Of your words
Drowning in the things you say
Going insane
Your pain
Your pleasure Heaven without measure
Sound and fury
Meaningless and signifying nothing

Different

We're different
Weird
We don't belong
But we're here
You can't deny it
You can't hide it
That we work different
And it's amazing
Don't think you're wrong
You're just changing
The rules
The world
Don't be ashamed to change how people think
And what they see
Just be yourself
You don't need help
You're not crazy
Just unique

Redemption

I should be ashamed God
Because I played a fake part and did what I wanted
And when I fell and plans failed I blamed you
Yet all the same in my sin and shame you remained
My hands were stained and yet
you sent your son to have his skin flayed and to be dishonored
But Lord I dishonored you and I
know your word says you forgive me
but I can't forgive myself. Every day I
feel I waste this life you give.
And though your word says you see all
I feel like I deceived you
When I prayed that I'd receive you and I said that I believe you
I still try to do it on my own but God I need you
You right next to me but for some reason I can't see you
Its because I'm steeped in my own stubbornness
But when I finally rest in you I feel your holiness.

Dream

I had a dream
So real I could grasp it
So vivid I could have it
Where I loved you
And you left me
To starve

Duality

Here I sit alone
I look at my clock
My mind starts to roam
It follows old paths
To a place I call home
It's a place that I go when I feel all alone
It's a twisted heaven
A frozen hell
A broken nirvana
A well furnished cell
Broken dreams and fractured hopes
Cracked concrete and broken ropes
Are All that hold this dying realm

Beneath The Oak Tree

I sit beneath the oak tree
And see
Softly hovering over the grasses
The mist flows over the earth like Clearing away the dust in my mind
Clearing the pain
The lies
The fails
The tries
It makes me think
That there's still a chance
for something
I smell the earth below me

The plants quietly growing
Holding the earth together
I hold the dust in my hands
And think
This is beautiful
I hear the rain falling
This is peace
As it breaks into a thousands pieces
Rolling down the leaves
Seeking to touch the earth
My mind is free
As I rest
Beneath the oak tree

Where Were You

You were not there when I needed you most
You were not there when I finally broke
You took the words that I said as a joke
You didn't know
You didn't know I was lonely
You didn't know I was only
Wanting a friend to know me

Wanting someone to show me
That I had a purpose
That I was not worthless
I try to perfect
I try to show you that I am not worthless
I'm doing all that I can
To show you that I really care
But you're not even there
Why do I bother to care
Why do I bother to try to be something for you that I'm not
Giving you all that I got
Working for what I don't got

Shadows

I never knew the noxious ways
You mind would work on me

Your creeping crawling running scrawling shadows follow me
Running racing raging chasing
Through these dusty streets
Filling feeding finding fear
I hid deep within me

Good Enough

I tired of people telling me what I can't do
Because when I am myself
They say oh no
That's not cool
I'm not here to be good for you
I'm not even here to be good for me
I'm just here to be honest
Weather I like it or not
I'm me
And I'm not free
Until I accept that I'm not free
That I am me
That I'm not in control
But you thinking that I am
It's getting old
I'm not sold
On societal expectations
Instead I'm searching for god's elevation
I'm seeking more than earthly sensations
I want to do more for our generation
So stop asking me to be something I'm not
Because being good for you
Just ain't my job

You

Your words hit me like gunfire
Burn me like sun fire
Your some liar
Turning me in circles
Working on my mind
Twisting my lines like a puppeteer
I fear you
You have such power over me
Your voice rings louder on my mind
Than any other
No other person can twist me like you
Corrupt me like you do
Like I knew
You would shoot me
And I took the bullet anyway
Hoping it wouldn't hurt me
It's not working
I try to cast you from my mind
But you're there all the time
The cause of my anxiety
I fear for you
Not me

Infinity

Here I stand if the water's edge
"Jump" the wind whispers gently
"Fly"
"I'll die" I cry
"Just try"
She sighs
Life, she explains
Is a risk you must take
It's a story you make
A chance to be great
But you're holding back
What you offer the world
When no one else is like you
No boy and no girl
Yes falling hurts
And maybe you'll cry
But you'll never know yourself
If you don't at least try
Fear can control you
Those lies can own you
But it's not you who made them
And those people don't know you
"I'm scared" I reply
Voice shaking in fear
"So are the eagles, they still fly my dear"
"But I'm still just a boy
My wings are not strong

All hope is lost
And my strength is all gone"
"Trust in the lord
And his love provides all
Now stop making excuses
you're ready to fall
You're ready to fail
For you must still learn
For The purest of knowledge is not taught, it's earned
So take that first leap
Let yourself change
You have everything to lose
But infinity to gain

Panic Attack

My heart is racing
Blood chasing
Lightning through my veins
I feel insane
I feel pain
I feel drained
Exhausted but awake
Out of breath but I can't take
A breath
Breathe
Be calm
Don't be alarmed
Don't be afraid
Just remain calm
Even though bombs
Explode beneath the skin
And I begin to panic
I feel fear
Like some horrible monster is near
I feel wrong
I feel awake to everything
But gone
A million miles away

Watching life play out from a Galaxy through a glass bottle
I can't breathe
I need
To breathe
I'm choking on air
Scared of nothing of something
Why
My mind is racing pacing chasing
Every horrible horrendous
Malignant possibility
Every fear and impossibility

I Hate You

I hate you
More than anything in this world
I hate you
For what you do to me
How you screw with me
It's cruelty
How you exert your control
Over me
Ending every thought of rebellion
Instead revering
You beauty
Your gruesome
Fiercely fearsome
Hateful
Graceful
Shameful
Jealousy

Insanity
Your broken and breaking me the same
We're twisted shadows
Rotted gallows
Two opponents alone
You and me
You are me
And despite how hard I try
We are one in the same

Paper Plane

God I know I'm supposed to be your creation but
Lately I've been feeling so deflated
I'm
Feeling worthless
Like I'm worth less
Than everyone else
And though I do my best
I can't keep up
Being
Beat up by myself
By my twisted shadows
In violent battles against my own psyche
Unlikely
To find peace
To he pleased in myself
I need your light in my life
I'm falling away
Floating away like a paper plane
Crumpled and forgotten in the wind
I've been gone

So long
So many things bother me
That I don't know what's actually wrong
Where it hurts
Deep seated pain
With roots as old as my birth
From the beginning of my time
Insecurities and fears
Hatred I've grown to love over the years
Sinister flowers deep rooted in my mind
Whispering lies
Covering my eyes
Keeping me blind
To see only what they see
Piloting this paper plane that is me

2:AM
It's 2:am and I'm exhausted
But I can't sleep
I can't keep
My eyes closed
As a silent wraith reaps my screaming mind
My manic thoughts don't know time
Know no time
Just my infinite span of thoughts
Every word I've got
Played back twice
No thrice
As I
Lie awake
Taking slow breaths to calm my moving mind
Taming a
Raging see
A hive of bees
A raging breeze
Blowing through trees
Shaking the foundations of earth itself
Shifting my reality
Breaking my sagacity
Lasting dreams
Rippling in my mind
Tearing the twine that

Holds me together
It's 2:am and thoughts roar in my head
Roam in my bed
Heavy like lead
But shapeless and void
Chaos contained in my head
All while I lay in my bed

Falling

She's falling
Plummeting from the sky
On bronze and wax wings
All the things
Weighing her down
She screams so loud
And makes no sound
She puts steel on her skin
Begging for help
A fragile porcelain doll
Falling from her shelf
Into her own personal hell
She spills her own blood hoping it will wake her
It's swallowed by darkness
She screams so loud
Yet makes no sound
No one to catch her
But friends all around

They tell her she's fine
Great advice
How profound
She screams in their windows
Slams on their doors
But when she opens her eyes
She six feet under their floorboards
She's dying
Can't you tell?
She tried to get help
But she still fell
She screams so loud
And makes no sound
As she lies
In blood soaked sand
Holding out her hand
To be helped
But no one's around
She screams so loud
She makes no sound
They say they never saw it
They couldn't tell
But if you really asked
She would tell
But no one cared
Or no one saw
They watched her fall but no one "saw"
She screamed so loud
But made no sound
If you listen close
The echo's still around
Still just as loud
Because she hasn't hit the ground
Someone can still save her
They just have to listen
To everything she's saying
Her fall is only beginning
Don't let her be another number
Another dead child
Don't let her be alone to fight life's trials
She screams so loud
And makes no sound

Perfect

Look in that mirror
What do you see
Every crack and flaw
All the things they don't see
How you
Can never be
Worthy
How you can never be
Anything
But worthless
Because the mirror can't lie

It screams that you're imperfect
The one curtain you can't hide behind
Is your own eye
That dark side
That keeps whispering
Like a broken record
Keeping every record of
You're imperfect form
Like a broken record playing
A record of every other person's words
Like a flock of birds
Incessantly screaming
Your too this
Not enough that
You're skinny
Your fat
You're wrong
Until the sound shattered your soul into sections
Into brittle prices
Full of infection
Drunk on fake love
High on the fumes of dead words
Craving another fix of self love
But surviving on cheap knockoffs of others affections
A chorus of birds screaming
If you look this way we'll love you
If you act this way we'll want you
But if you don't behave well shun you
We want to be
Perfect

Addicted To Rage

He's got a look in his eye
Blind rage
He's caged for so long

Seductive sirens
Scream their songs
In his ear
His fists curl
Until his nails bite his skin
He begins to bleed
But he doesn't see
He doesn't notice
That he's losing control
While he's blood screams through his bloodstreams
He can hear his mind speak
But doesn't know what it means
He's angry
Enraged
But this pain is euphoric
It's addicting
This anger
Holding this hate
Feels amazing
He feels powerful
Like he can lift mountains
Turn rivers
Into fountains
Wield the sun in his hands
And never burn
But he'll never learn
After the anger is gone
The sun always burns
Cause once the adrenalines gone all that's left is the hurt
And hiding with anger will just make that hurt worse
Rage in itself is a dangerous emotion
And the pain it will cause you is enough to drown oceans
And when fights break out that way it leaves both sides broken
Now both parties hold hatred
For the joy that was stolen
But the fire that they started didn't have to keep rising
But because they're both stubborn
Both are crying

Anew

Run
Take up your things
And run
From life
Strife
Escape your reality
On winged sandals
Fly away
And dream
Glide into the night
On bronze and wax wings
Let nothing
Hold you down
Just close your eyes and fly
Let their words slide off of you
Shed like a second skin
And be yourself
Shine
Like the moon on a black night sky
Unashamed
Unafraid
Take to the night sky with inked wings
Write the stars into place
Dance them into submission
Sing the raging waves to sleep
And write them a universe of their own
Write your own world
To call home
And fly on those empty skies and fill them
With wonder
Tear that broken earth asunder
And build upon it
Anew

Lonely

I check my phone
Nothing
No ones home
Just me
This silence is crippling
Like heavy iron weights on my spine
Leaving my mind blank
Save for one thing
The loneliness
The silence won't go unheard
My mind reeling at the lack of words
Flying in the air like birds
Relaying messages to my mind
As my mind responds in time like a song meant for two
Truly
Alone
Silence screaming to me
As my soul is emptied
Because no one remembers me
I'm forgotten
Alone

In this broken silence
I'm forced to remember
That I am nothing
That the world spins wildly and out of control weather I sit upon it's glass shard throne or not
I am no king
I am a ronin
Nothing without a people
Longing to belong for so long
That my mind is slowly gone
And as this begins to process
Cracks appear in the glass of my reality
Lying sagaciously
Screaming hatefully into the void
As my shards
Fall alongside
Me
Making shapes in the ashes and fine glass dust

High School

Wake up
And we
Strap on out paper armor
Armed and ready for the day
Another day at war
In the trenches
With our bows strapped to our back
Ready at a moment's notice to fight back
See this is not a place of education
This is a sacred battleground
With flaming arrows flying by
Ready to rend our ripened flesh
And pillage and raid our minds
A thousand enemies surrounding us all of us thinking the same,

Not me first,
One hand on our blades at all times
Prepared to siphon souls from shallow waiting warriors
We're not evil, we just want to survive
We want to appear strong to protect ourselves from the wolves that surround us
So we say what we have to
No matter how bad it sounds
We loose flaming arrows into each other's side
Until both on both sides
Are sitting alone at home screaming into the void
For help
Because we push each other to the point
That suicide seems like the answer
And the wounds get infected and spread like a cancer through the body and leaps from man to man to woman on infectious breaths and poisoned blades
Drinking away our being until all we have left is shades
This is not a school, it's a war zone and all of us are landmines waiting to explode
Like landlines
Transporting pain through each other's airwaves
All of us insane
Paranoid of each other's words

Lone Wolves

The lonely wolf screams to the night
To mask his hollow pain
He knows the danger of lonely wolves but he's lonely all the same
His hallowed hardened hidden heart
Is buried deep within
He tries to mask his loneliness
But cannot keep it in

The violent silence screaming out
Echoes in his ears
It never falters
Never flees
It simply screams it's silent noise
Whispers Dreams of hostile void
Flinging shadows
Across my eye

Self Worth

Self worth
How do I measure this
Do I measure it in measurements
In the inches I count on my waist
Or the shoes I wear or my subscriber base
How do I prove to the world that I matter
With Instagram followers and snapchat views
The number of numbers I have in my phone
Or the times I'm left on read when I feel alone
Is it
How many people claim to be my friends
Although most of them leave me before my struggle ends
Is it
How many girls I can pull on the street
Or how boys look at her
That attention that we seek
Is my value measured in money
Something tangible to attain
How many words I write
The pictures I can paint
Is my value of value to you
Is what I'm trying to say
Or what must I do to prove
What must I do to be saved
To show that I'm human
Do I have to dance good or sing good or look good or act good
Because I want to be bad
I want to scream and shout on rooftops of my pain
I want to scream until I no longer feel insane
I want to be me
I want my value to have value in this world without compromising myself or my beliefs
I want to be free to feel joy or feel grief
Not this miasma of false joy we all use to mask the same pain

Fake Friends

Are you really my friend?
Like from now till the end
Cause I have nothing else to offer
except that I have your back
But do you have mine cause time and time again people prove that they are incapable of truth that the people we trust are just slipping in snakeskin
Waiting for the right time to strike
Like a plague I can't escape
I can't tell who's fake
It's scary
Because If I trust the wrong man I put a knife in his hands and tell him stab me
And that's what it's like loving fake people
Thinking that they love you but their intentions are evil
Your waiting for them to dig you out of your grave not knowing they the ones filling it in the first place
This is what it's like needing something to survive and at the same times its killing you with lies by god is this all we can do
I'm loosing my ability to trust and I'm too scared to love
I'm backed against the walls because I been back stabbed too many times by all the
People I've trusted b
Because it wasn't my love they wanted
But for my usefulness they lusted and when their agendas are fulfilled they leave you to be killed or do the killing themselves
See not everyone behind you is really behind you and when you fall it becomes a race to see who
Is going to stab you first
Your brothers
Your sisters
roaring toward you like twisters tearing you down from the inside
They say keep your friends close and your enemies closer but I feel like it would be better if I was just alone and I know that I'm on my own and safe away from the people who want to break me and take me to those dark places and they know all my weak spaces that I let them expose and I tell them my business

just to be exposed as soon as we argue

And you can't argue because you know it's true

When your back is turned they have so much to say about you

And your flaws

And problems

So part of me says forget all them

But it is not good for man to be alone

But I'm afraid to be hurt if i don't stay separated

Gone

Apart from the whole

Hiding from everyone I know

I don't want to go and be hurt again

So no, I don't want friends and I don't trust you

Because I know you before you know me and I know the things that your wanting and I refuse to be used

To lose

I'm not going to be another idiot who trusted too much

But if you ever need me

I got you.

Why It Still Hurts

Words long since faded to dust
Long forgotten
Yet they remain in my mind
All the time
It still hurts
It's been so long
But those words
Still play over and over again in my mind
All the time
When sleep
When I eat
When I look in the mirror
The voice becomes clearer
Staring back at me
Taunting me to move
Saying
Stop me
Take control
But I can't
Because words have great power untold
Unknown
The power of life and death is in the tongue
Every word a spear
Each syllable an arrow
Screaming through the air
Hissing in my ear
Telling me all the things I hide
All the things I don't want to hear
My fear
Anger anxiety
Secrets that I'm hiding
Exposed to me
I can lie no longer to myself
I'm forced to face hell itself
My own mind

Will I Change

I once was asked
By a friend of mine
Who I would become
If given time
I sat for a while
Giving it thought
As time moved on
Would I not
Still be the same me
Still dreaming the same dreams
Because all these years
It always seemed
That although I grow
I'd never change
I'd get more mature
But stay the same
But like Theseus's ship
Always broken then fixed
Eventually my claim
That I'll always be the same
Would become
Nothing more
Than an optimistic lie
Just a chance to deny what I know
That I won't
Always be the same
Yet perhaps it may be
That this is a good thing

Hope Is A Lie

The truth is a blinding light
Shining over an ocean of lies
Gliding on black skies
On wings of fear and rage
It's a rushing river that empties lakes
A hungry beast that takes and takes
A monster that terrifies
An ever living hawk
Scouting the skies
Bringing death to all
Because hope is the ultimate lie
A lie that lives on as long as the light is gone
Hope survives when hidden from the truth
Hope is the noble lie staying my soul from chaos and rage
Hope is a cage
Hope is control
Hope is a blinder over my eyes
And now that hope is gone
And all that's left is an infinite
Black void through which I cannot find my way
Without my hope
Without my faith I stumble even though my eyes are open and my path is empty
I am blind to trouble

Though I see
Everything

My Sister At The Edge Of The Bar

To my sister at the edge of the bar
Thank you
For just a moment while you were there
I felt myself
Something no one else has done for me
I won't remember your name
But I'll never forget your voice as you sang
Or your smile
Or the look in your eye as your hand graced the worn cardboard and gave this world life and light
The way you lit up and said you were an art teacher
And I saw something pure
Love
You still made me smile
A real smile
For a while.
For those brief two hours
With my phone nearly dead and no internet to hide behind
You wiped my tears away
You made me feel alright

I had buried my heart
But you showed me the sky
And every word my hand has uttered since
Is inspired by your smile
And your voice
Your kind eyes searching mine
As you sought to see my heart
And understood my pain
Like no one else before you
You gave my life value
You gave my words meaning
You made me feel like something
When I had been living so long as nothing
I was trapped at the bottom of a well
And your slurred words lifted me
And I couldn't help but feel shy
When with a shaking voice I asked you why
You wanted my scrawled picture of a fox
Lazily drawn on a cardboard box
You took the worn down thing in your hands
And explained
That you thought my work and my words were magnificent
And I said a shaky thank you
And I must admit a tear left my eye
When you took my hand, hugged me, and said goodbye
And I hope to God that I'll see you again
The woman who made me smile again
My sister
At the edge of the bar

Made in the USA
San Bernardino,
CA